SCHOLASTIC

Let's Find Out

My REBUS Reader

Feelings at School

by Patrick Walker

SCHOLASTIC INC.
New York Toronto London Auckland Sydney New Delhi Hong Kong

You may feel  at school.

happy

You may feel  at school.

sad

You may feel 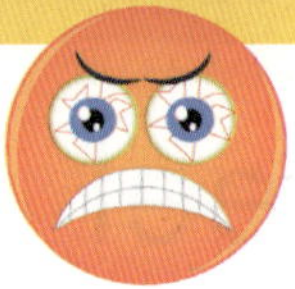 at school.

angry

You may feel  at school.

nervous

You may feel  at school.

proud

You may feel  at school.

excited

How do these kids feel?